Cords & Bling JEWELRY

A little bling goes a long way in creating impressive cord jewelry! See what happens with these bracelets, necklaces, and earrings when you add just a few glitzy beads, charms, or closures. The results are simply fabulous!

2

4

5

6

8

10

12

13

14

16

18

20

22

25

26

27

LEISURE ARTS, INC. • Maumelle, Arkansas

Zigzag Bracelet

SHOPPING LIST

- ☐ 4 yards of purple braiding cord
- ☐ 10 mm beads (we used 20)

TO MAKE THE BRACELET:

1. Cut the thread into two 72" long lengths. Holding the ends together, fold the cords in half. Tie an overhand knot (page 32) about 3/4" from the fold; tape down the knot.
2. Use the two outer cords to tie two square knots (page 32) around the two center cords.
3. Thread a bead on the left outer cord and tie the first half of a square knot.
4. Thread a bead on the right outer cord and tie the second half of a square knot. Tie another square knot.
5. Repeat Steps 3-4 until the bracelet is the desired length.
6. Tie an overhand knot close to the last square knot and trim the cords about 3" from the knot.

Ladder Bracelet

SHOPPING LIST

- ☐ 4 yards of aqua braiding cord
- ☐ 10 mm faceted beads (we used 22)

TO MAKE THE BRACELET:

1. Cut the cord into two 72" long lengths. Holding the ends together, fold the cords in half. Tie an overhand knot (page 32) about 3/4" from the fold; tape down the knot.
2. Use the two outer cords to tie two square knots (page 32) around the two center cords.
3. Thread one bead on each of the outer cords and tie 2 square knots.
4. Repeat Step 3 until bracelet is the desired length.
5. Tie an overhand knot close to the last square knot and trim the cords about 3" from the knot.

Button Bracelet

SHOPPING LIST

- ☐ $4^1/_2$ yards of silver metallic braiding cord
- ☐ 1" dia. two-hole button
- ☐ silver bead

Approximate finished length: *$7^1/_2$"*

TO MAKE THE BRACELET:

1. Cut four 36" lengths and one 18" length of cord. Holding one end of all five cords together, tie an overhand knot (page 32) about 2" from one end; tape down the knot.
2. Use the four longer outer cords to tie 17 square knots (page 32) around the shorter center cord.
3. Slide the button and the bead on the short center cord and tie 17 square knots.
4. Tie an overhand knot close to the last square knot and trim the cords about 2" from the knot.

The length of the finished bracelet can be adjusted by tying more or less knots at the beginning and the end.

Tube Bead Necklace & Bracelet

The necklace and the bracelet are made in the same manner. The numbers given in parentheses refer to the bracelet.

SHOPPING LIST

- ☐ 17" (7 1/2") length **each** of 3 colors of braiding cord
- ☐ silver foldover cord ends
- ☐ 3 (3) silver tube beads
- ☐ 12 (6) 4 mm silver beads
- ☐ 6 8 mm turquoise beads (for necklace only)
- ☐ silver lobster clasps
- ☐ silver jump rings
- ☐ jeweler's glue
- ☐ chain-nose pliers (2 pairs)

Approximate necklace finished length: 17 1/2"

Approximate bracelet finished length: 8"

TO MAKE THE NECKLACE AND BRACELET:

1. Attach one foldover cord end (page 31) to one end of all braiding cord lengths.
2. Slide 1 tube bead, 4 (2) silver beads, and 2 turquoise beads (for necklace only) on each braiding cord length.
3. Repeat Step 1 at the opposite end of the cord lengths.
4. Use the jump rings (page 30) to attach the clasp to one foldover cord end. Attach a jump ring to the other foldover cord end.

Triple-Wrap Bracelet

SHOPPING LIST

- ☐ 1 3/4 yards of bronze leather cord
- ☐ 7/8" bronze flower-shaped shank-style button
- ☐ 4 yards of Beadalon® 7 strand silver bead stringing wire
- ☐ bronze and silver beads (we used 83)
- ☐ wire cutters
- ☐ tape

TO MAKE THE BRACELET:

1. Cut a 60" length of cord. Fold the cord in half. Use a lark's head knot (page 31) to attach the fold to the button shank.
2. Fold wire in half. Wrap fold of wire around leather cords about 1/4" below knot. Tape down the button. Tape the leather cord ends down.
3. Bring the wire ends behind the cords and pass the wire ends through a bead from opposite directions ***(Fig. 1)***.

Fig. 1

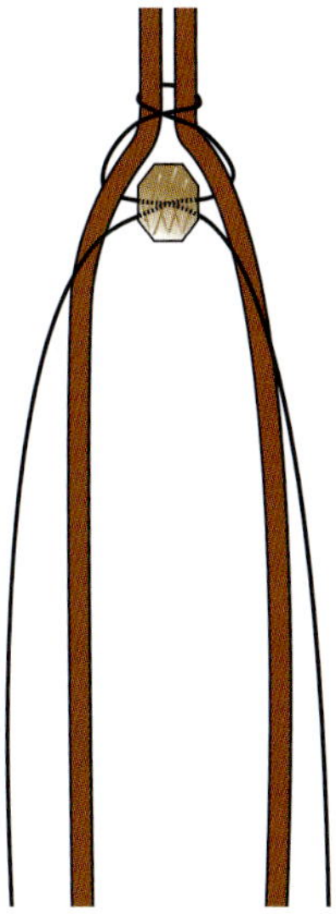

4. Wrapping the wire behind the cords, add another bead as you did in Step 3 ***(Fig. 2)***.

Fig. 2

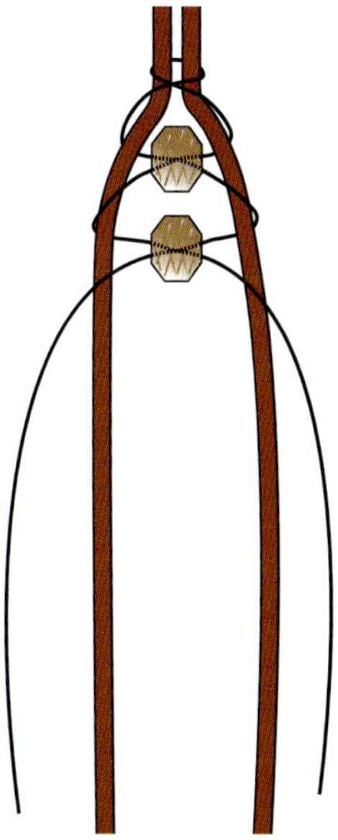

5. Repeat Step 3 until the bracelet is the right length when wrapped around your wrist three times. Wrap the wire around the cords below the last bead; trim the wire ends.
6. To make the button loop, tie an overhand knot (page 32) with the cords approximately 1" below the secured wire. Check to see that the button will fit through the loop. Trim the ends of the cords.

Dangle Bracelet

SHOPPING LIST

- ☐ 3/4 yard of green satin rat tail cord
- ☐ silver foldover cord ends
- ☐ silver toggle clasp
- ☐ 2 silver metal beads
- ☐ 7 assorted beads for dangles
- ☐ silver head pins
- ☐ silver jump rings
- ☐ jeweler's glue
- ☐ chain-nose pliers, round-nose pliers, and wire cutters

TO MAKE THE BRACELET:

1. Measure your wrist and decide how loose or tight you want your bracelet; subtract 1". Cut three cords this length.
2. Make seven bead dangles (page 30) with beads and head pins.
3. Attach one foldover cord end (page 31) to one end of each cord length.
4. Use a jump ring (page 30) to attach one clasp end to the foldover cord ends. Slide one metal bead on all three cord lengths. Slide two bead dangles on each of two cords and three bead dangles on the remaining cord. Slide the remaining metal bead on all three cords.
5. Attach foldover cord ends to the opposite end of the cord lengths.
6. Use a jump ring to attach the remaining clasp end to the foldover cord ends.

Beaded Bracelet

SHOPPING LIST

- ☐ 1/4 yard **each** of pink and grey satin rat tail cord
- ☐ 12 mm long silver metal beads (we used 9)
- ☐ 4 mm pink beads (we used 20)
- ☐ silver foldover cord ends
- ☐ silver toggle clasp
- ☐ silver nylon-coated beading wire
- ☐ silver jump rings
- ☐ silver crimp beads and crimp tool
- ☐ jeweler's glue
- ☐ chain-nose pliers and wire cutters

TO MAKE THE BRACELET:

1. Measure your wrist and decide how loose or tight you want your bracelet; subtract 1". Cut two cord lengths the determined measurement.
2. Attach one foldover cord end (page 31) to each end of each cord length.
3. Cut 1 piece of wire 12" long.
4. Use a crimp bead (page 30) to attach the wire length to one jump ring. Thread the beads on the wire until the beads are the length determined in Step 1. Use a crimp bead to attach the wire end to another jump ring.
5. Open the jump ring (page 30) on one end of the beaded strand and attach one end of each cord and one clasp end to the jump ring. Repeat at the opposite end.

Heart Necklace

SHOPPING LIST

- ☐ 5 yards of dark pink satin rat tail cord
- ☐ silver heart pendant
- ☐ 4 metal-lined large-hole beads (2 pink and 2 pink crystal)
- ☐ 2 large-hole silver spacer beads
- ☐ decorative "S" clasp
- ☐ large jump ring
- ☐ craft glue

Approximate finished length: 22", excluding pendant

TO MAKE THE NECKLACE:

1. Cut two 12" lengths of cord; set aside. Cut the remaining cord into three cords 52" long. Holding the cords together, slide the pendant to the center of the cords. Tape the pendant down.
2. Working one side of the necklace at a time, use two outer cords to loosely tie a square knot (page 32) around the center cord.
3. Slide one pink bead onto the cords. Tie two square knots about 1" from the first square knot.
4. Slide 1 crystal bead onto the cords. Tie two square knots about 1" from the last square knot.
5. Slide a spacer bead onto the cords. Trim the cord ends $8^1/_4$" from the last knot.
6. Repeat Steps 2-5 for the opposite side of the necklace.
7. Finish the cord ends (page 31) using the 12" cord lengths and the jump ring on one end and the "S" clasp on the other end.

Angel Wings Necklace

SHOPPING LIST

- ☐ 5 yards of grey satin rat tail cord
- ☐ silver angel wing pendant
- ☐ 4 metal-lined large-hole beads (2 grey & 2 crystal)
- ☐ 2 large-hole silver spacer beads
- ☐ decorative "S" clasp
- ☐ large jump ring
- ☐ craft glue

Approximate finished length: 27", excluding pendant

TO MAKE THE NECKLACE:

1. Cut two 12" lengths of cord; set aside. Cut the remaining cord into three cords 52" long. Holding the cords together, slide the pendant to the center of the cords. Tape the pendant down.
2. Slide one grey bead onto the cords. Working one side of the necklace at a time and beginning approximately $^3/_4$" below the bead, use two outer cords to loosely tie two square knots (page 32) around the center cord.
3. Slide 1 crystal bead onto the cords. Tie 2 square knots about $1^1/_2$" from the last square knot.
4. Slide a spacer bead onto the cords. Trim the cord ends $10^1/_2$" from the last knot.
5. Repeat Steps 2-4 for the opposite side of the necklace.
6. Finish the cord ends (page 31) using the 12" cord lengths and the jump ring on one end and the "S" clasp on the other end.

Leather Cord & Bling Bracelet

SHOPPING LIST

- ☐ 1 yard of leather cord
- ☐ 2 metal-lined, large-hole rhinestone beads
- ☐ 3 silver spacers
- ☐ silver toggle clasp
- ☐ craft glue

TO MAKE THE BRACELET:

1. Cut the cord into two 18" lengths. Holding the ends together, fold the cords in half. Use a lark's head knot (page 31) to attach the cords to the ring on one toggle clasp piece.
2. Refer to **Fig. 1** to thread a spacer onto the cords.

Fig. 1

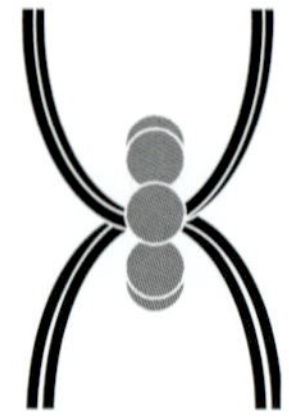

3. Alternating the beads and spacers, repeat Step 2 to thread 2 beads and 2 spacers onto the cords.
4. Tie the cords to the remaining toggle clasp piece at the desired length; trim ends. Place a drop of glue on the knot; allow to dry. Slide beads and spacers along the cords until they are evenly spaced.

Pearls & Rhinestone Choker

SHOPPING LIST

- ☐ 6 yards pink braiding cord that will fit through the beads
- ☐ 17" rhinestone chain with eyelet ends
- ☐ 4 mm pink pearl beads (we used 170)
- ☐ silver lobster clasp
- ☐ silver jump rings
- ☐ chain-nose pliers (2 pairs)
- ☐ craft glue

Approximate finished length: 17"

TO MAKE THE CHOKER:

1. Attach the lobster clasp to one end of the chain using a jump ring (page 30). Attach a jump ring to the remaining end.
2. Beginning with the center of the cord below the jump ring, knot the cord around the chain.
3. Slide one bead onto each cord; tie a square knot (page 32) around the chain in the space below the first rhinestone.
4. Continue adding beads and tying square knots in the spaces between the rhinestones until you reach the last rhinestone; knot the ends above the jump ring. Place a drop of glue on the cord ends. When the glue is dry, trim the cord ends.

Tassel Necklace & Earrings

Both of these necklace and earring sets are made the same way and the look is easily changed just by using different colors of cords and beads.

SHOPPING LIST

- ☐ $3^1/_2$ yards of braiding cord
- ☐ assorted small beads
- ☐ assorted large beads
- ☐ 2 ear wires

Approximate finished necklace length: *24"*

TO MAKE THE NECKLACE:

1. Cut three 36" lengths of cord. Holding the ends together, tie an overhand knot (page 32) at the center of the cords.
2. Beginning approximately $7^1/_2$"-$9^1/_2$" from the knot, tie an overhand knot, slide on a small bead, and tie another overhand knot on each strand as desired.
3. Holding all the cords together, tie an overhand knot about 12" from the first overhand knot.
4. Thread two small beads and a large bead on each cord end and tie an overhand knot at the end of each cord as desired. Trim the cord ends as desired.

TO MAKE THE EARRINGS:

1. Cut the cord into two 8" long lengths.
2. Insert one cord through an ear wire; fold the cord in half.
3. Thread a small bead over both cord ends up to the ear wire.
4. Thread two small beads and a large bead on each cord end and tie an overhand knot (page 32) at the end of each cord as desired. Trim the cord ends as desired.

Rhinestone & Paracord Bracelet

SHOPPING LIST

- ☐ 1/2 yard of paracord
- ☐ 4" rhinestone chain
- ☐ metallic braiding cord
- ☐ large eye hand sewing needle
- ☐ very large silver lobster clasp
- ☐ hot glue gun and gluesticks
- ☐ charm, silver jump ring, and chain-nose pliers (optional)

TO MAKE THE BRACELET:

1. Measure your wrist and decide how loose or tight you want your bracelet; subtract 1". Multiply the determined measurement by 2. Cut the paracord this length.
2. Slide the lobster clasp on one end of the paracord. Fold the end of the paracord over about 3/4" and glue to the opposite end of the paracord, forming a loop.

3. Thread each needle with an 18" length of braiding cord; knot the ends. Beginning on the end opposite the clasp and about 1¹/₄" below the end, sew through the paracord with one needle from each side.
4. Center the rhinestone chain between the paracord loop.
5. Wrap the left braiding cord around the chain below the first rhinestone *(Fig. 1)*.

Fig. 1

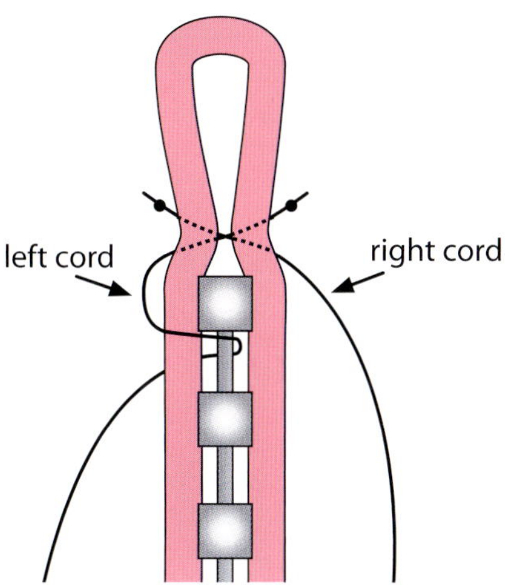

6. Wrap the right braiding cord around the chain below the first rhinestone *(Fig. 2)*.

Fig. 2

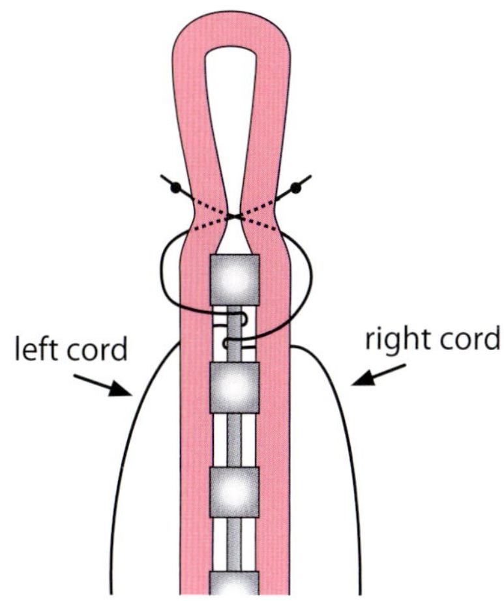

7. Repeat Steps 5-6 along the length of the rhinestone chain. After the last rhinestone, insert the needles through the paracord and knot; trim the braiding cord ends.
8. Cut two 16" lengths of braiding cord. Finish the ends (page 31), wrapping the braiding cord lengths between the chain ends and the lobster clasp and loop.
9. If desired, use a jump ring (page 30) to attach the charm to the loop end.

Paracord & Beads Bracelet

SHOPPING LIST

- ☐ three 5" lengths of assorted pink paracord
- ☐ 2 metal spacers
- ☐ 2 silver metal cones
- ☐ stretch cord
- ☐ 10 mm pink faceted beads (we used 9)
- ☐ bead for bead stop
- ☐ 24 gauge wire
- ☐ round-nose pliers and wire cutters
- ☐ jeweler's glue

Approximate finished length: *8"*

TO MAKE THE BRACELET:

1. Holding the ends together, tightly wrap a 6" wire length around the paracord *(Fig. 1)*.

Fig. 1

2. Thread the wire end through a cone. Place a generous drop of glue on the cord ends. Pull the wire until the wrapped paracord ends are drawn into the cone *(Fig. 2)*. Trim the wire to 1/2". Make a loop in the wire (page 30).

Fig. 2

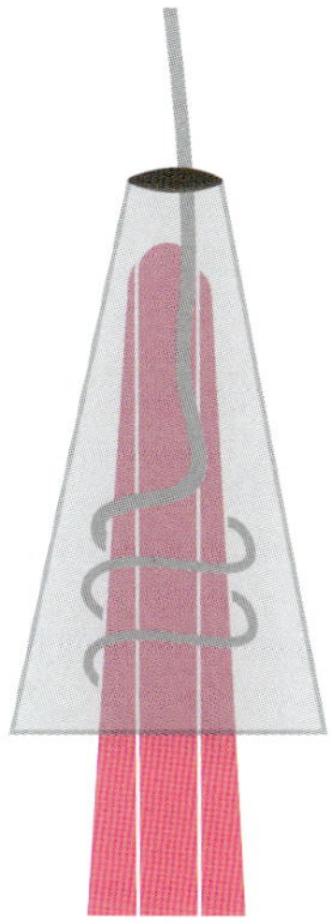

3. Slide the spacers on the paracord lengths.
4. Repeat Steps 1-2 for the remaining paracord ends.
5. Using a bead stop (page 29), thread the beads on an 8" length of stretch cord.
6. Tie one end of the stretch cord to one wire loop using a surgeon's knot (page 32) and apply a drop of glue to the knot. Once dry, trim the stretch cord ends.
7. Check the bracelet size, adding or removing beads until the bracelet is the right length. Remove the bead stop. Tie the remaining end of the stretch cord to the remaining wire loop using a surgeon's knot. Apply glue to the knot and allow to dry. Once dry, trim the stretch cord ends.

Paracord Cuff

SHOPPING LIST

- ☐ 7 feet **each** of teal and yellow paracord
- ☐ very large silver lobster clasp
- ☐ craft glue

TO MAKE THE BRACELET:

The "working" cord is the cord you are using at the time in each step.

1. Measure your wrist and decide how loose or tight you want your bracelet; add 5". Holding the two cords side-by-side, measure from one end of the cords to the determined measurement. Hold the cords at this point.
2. Fold the ends of the cords over to the right and match the ends with the marked point. To make the loop, drop the yellow cord down in front of the teal cord about 3/4" *(Fig. 1)*.
3. Fold the right end of the teal working cord over the left end of both cords *(Fig. 2)*.
4. Bring the teal working cord around the back of the loop *(Fig. 3)* to the front of the loop and through the loop made by the teal working cord *(Fig. 4)*. Tighten the cords, leaving about a 1/2" green loop at the top.
5. *You may find it helpful to tape the loop down when working.* Loop the right end of the yellow working cord under the two center cords and over the teal left outer cord *(Fig. 5)*.
6. Loop the teal left working cord to the right, over the yellow vertical cord, under the yellow horizontal cord above it, over the teal vertical cord, and under the right yellow loop *(Fig. 6)*; tighten slightly.

7. Loop the teal right working cord to the left, over both the vertical cords, and under the yellow left working cord *(Fig. 7)*.
8. Loop the yellow left working cord to the right, under the yellow vertical cord, over the teal horizontal cord above it, under the teal vertical cord, and over the right teal loop *(Fig. 8)*; tighten slightly.
9. Repeat Steps 5-8 until a minimum of 5" of cord ends remain. Tie the first half of a square knot (page 32) *(Fig. 9)*. Then tie a square knot (page 32).
10. Slide the clasp on the long teal cord *(Fig. 10)*. Trim all cords to approximately 4" . Tuck the ends of the cords under the cords on the back of the bracelet *(Fig. 11)*. Trim the ends close and place glue on the ends; allow to dry.

Fig. 1

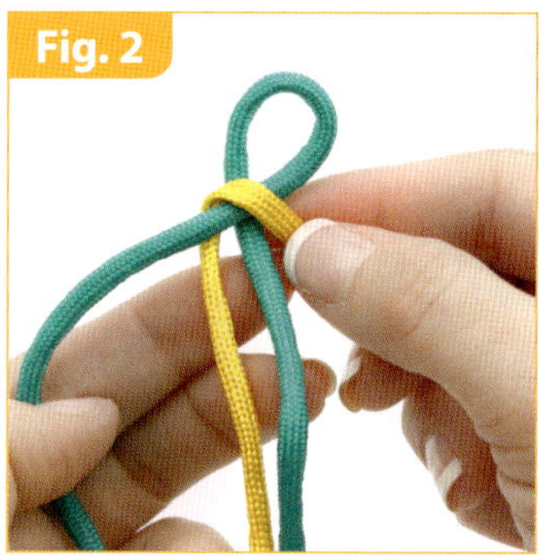
Fig. 2

Fig. 3

Fig. 4

Fig. 5

Fig. 6

Fig. 7

Fig. 8

Fig. 9

Fig. 10

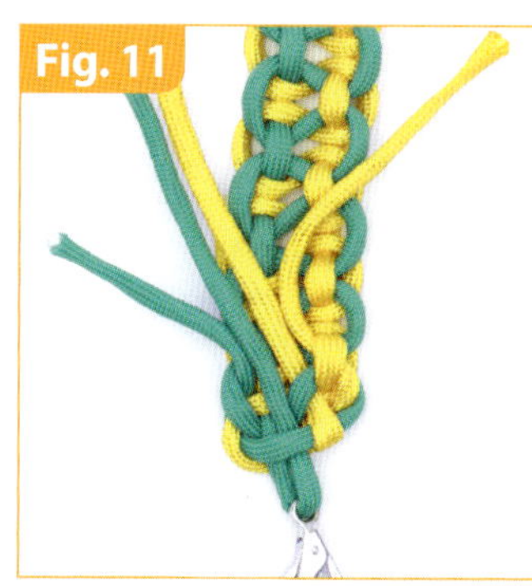
Fig. 11

Love Necklace

SHOPPING LIST

- ☐ 4 yards of lavender braiding cord
- ☐ "Love" pendant
- ☐ two 6 mm silver beads
- ☐ eighteen 6 mm crystal bicone beads
- ☐ silver foldover cord ends
- ☐ silver lobster clasp
- ☐ silver jump rings
- ☐ chain-nose pliers
- ☐ jeweler's glue

Approximate finished length: 18"

TO MAKE THE NECKLACE:

1. Cut the cord into four 36" lengths.
2. Insert two cords through the ring on the "E" end of the pendant. Center the pendant on the cords. Use the two outside cords to tie two square knots (page 32) around the two center cords. Tape the pendant down.
3. Using the three cords on the right, slide a bicone bead on the right center cord; tie a square knot.
4. Still using the three cords on the right, slide a bicone bead on the left cord; tie a square knot.
5. Repeat Steps 3-4 for a total of 9 bicone beads. Tie two square knots. Slide on a silver bead and tie an overhand knot (page 32) just below the bead.
6. Insert two cords through the ring on the "L" end of the pendant. Center the pendant on the cords. Use the two outside cords to tie two square knots around the two center cords.
7. Using the three cords on the left, slide a bicone bead on the left center cord; tie a square knot.
8. Still using the three cords on the left, slide a bicone bead on the right cord; tie a square knot.
9. Repeat Steps 7-8 for a total of 9 bicone beads. Tie two square knots. Slide on a silver bead and tie an overhand knot just below the bead.
10. Trim the cord ends 4" from the overhand knots. Attach a foldover cord end (page 31) to each group of cords.
11. Use a jump ring (page 30) to attach the foldover cord end to a lobster clasp on one end. Attach another jump ring to the remaining foldover cord end.

Peace Necklace

SHOPPING LIST

- ☐ 4 yards of turquoise braiding cord
- ☐ "Peace" pendant
- ☐ two 6 mm silver beads
- ☐ sixteen 3 mm seed beads
- ☐ silver foldover cord ends
- ☐ silver lobster clasp
- ☐ silver jump rings

Approximate finished length: 18"

TO MAKE THE NECKLACE:

1. Cut the cord into four 36" long lengths.
2. Insert two cords through the ring on the "P" end of the pendant. Center the pendant on the cords. Use the two outside cords to tie two square knots (page 32) around the two center cords. Tape the pendant down.
3. Using the three cords on the right, slide a seed bead on the center cord and the right cord; tie a square knot.

Continued on page 24.

Peace Necklace continued.

4. Using the three cords on the left, slide a seed bead on the center cord and left cord; tie two square knots.
5. Using the three cords on the right, slide 2 seed beads on the center cord; tie two square knots.
6. Using the three cords on the left, slide a seed bead on the center cord; tie a square knot.
7. Using the three cords on the right, slide a seed bead on the center cord; tie a square knot.
8. Slide a silver bead on all four cords and tie an overhand knot (page 32) just below the bead.
9. Insert two cords through the ring on the "E" end of the pendant. Center the pendant on the cords. Use the two outside cords to tie two square knots around the two inside cords.
10. Using the three cords on the left, slide a seed bead on the center cord and left cord; tie a square knot.
11. Using the three cords on the right, slide a seed bead on the center cord and right cord; tie two square knots.
12. Using the three cords on the left, slide two seed beads on the center cord; tie two square knots.
13. Using the three cords on the right, slide a seed bead on the center cord; tie a square knot.
14. Using the three cords on the left, slide a seed bead on the center cord; tie a square knot.
15. Slide a silver bead on all four cords and tie an overhand knot just below the bead.
16. Trim the cord ends $5^1/_2$" from the overhand knots. Attach a foldover cord end (page 31) to each group of cords.
17. Use a jump ring (page 30) to attach the foldover cord end to a lobster clasp on one end. Attach another jump ring to the remaining foldover cord end.

Pearl Pendant Necklace

SHOPPING LIST

- ☐ 3 3/8 yards natural color hemp cord
- ☐ 2 1/2" long gold and pearl pendant with jump ring
- ☐ 8 10 mm x 15 mm fresh water pearl beads
- ☐ 16 3 mm gold seed beads
- ☐ gold toggle clasp
- ☐ craft glue
- ☐ chain-nose pliers (2 pair)

Approximate finished length: 18", excluding pendant

TO MAKE THE NECKLACE:

1. Cut two 36" lengths, one 18" length, and two 12" lengths of braiding cord.
2. Holding the three longer lengths together, thread the cord ends through the ring on one toggle clasp piece. Finish the cord ends (page 31).
3. Using the longer cords for the outer cords and the short cord for the center cord, tie 21 square knots (page 32).
4. Slide one fresh water pearl and 2 seed beads on the center cord. Tie 10 square knots.
5. Repeat Step 4 seven times.
6. Tie 11 more square knots.
7. Repeat Step 2 to attach the cords to the remaining toggle clasp piece.
8. Use the jump ring (page 30) to attach the pendant to the center of the necklace.

Cross Bracelet

SHOPPING LIST

- ☐ 6 yards of purple braiding cord
- ☐ $1^1/_4$"w x $1^3/_4$"l rhinestone cross with back loops
- ☐ 6 silver spacers
- ☐ 2 decorative silver cones
- ☐ silver toggle clasp
- ☐ craft glue

Approximate finished length: *8"*

TO MAKE THE NECKLACE:

1. Cut the cord into six 36" long lengths.
2. Insert three cords through one ring on the back of the cross; center the cross on the cords. Using two cords as a single cord, use the outer cords to tie two square knots (page 32) around the two center cords.
3. Slide three spacers onto the cords.
4. Tie five square knots.
5. Slide a cone and a clasp end on the cords. Thread the cords back through the cone. Tie an overhand knot (page 32) around all six cords as close as possible to the upper end of the cone. Apply glue to the knot. Once dry, trim the cord ends close to the knot.
6. Repeat Steps 2-5 for the remaining side of the bracelet.

Beaded Cuff

SHOPPING LIST

- ☐ $15\frac{1}{4}$ yards of black braiding cord that will fit through the beads
- ☐ 8 mm beads (we used 43 assorted color beads for our 8" bracelet)
- ☐ toggle clasp
- ☐ 2 decorative metal cones
- ☐ silver jump rings
- ☐ 24 gauge wire
- ☐ round nose pliers and wire cutters
- ☐ craft glue

TO MAKE THE BRACELET:

1. Measure the length of the closed clasp and both cones. Subtract this total measurement from the desired finished length.
2. Cut six 78" lengths and five 15" lengths of braiding cord. Holding the ends together, tie a loose overhand knot (page 32) about $\frac{1}{2}$" from one end. Tape the knot down.
3. Arrange the cords as shown in Fig. 1.

Fig. 1

L = long
S = short

4. The knots are tied using a group of three cords. In a group, the short cord is the center cord that the knots are tied around. Using cord 1, 2, and 3, tie three square knots (page 32). Using cords 5, 6, and 7, tie three square knots. Using cords 9, 10, and 11, tie three square knots.

5. Using cords 3, 4, and 5, tie three square knots. Using cords 7, 8, and 9, tie three square knots. Slide a bead on cords 2, 6, and 10 *(Fig. 2)*.

Fig. 2

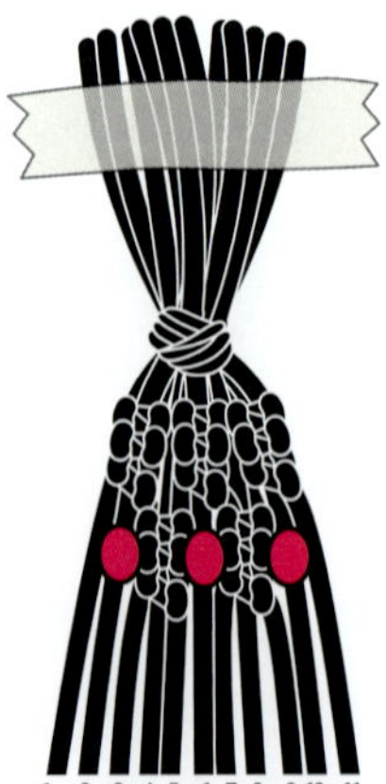

6. Using cords 1, 2, and 3, tie three square knots. Using cords 5, 6, and 7, tie three square knots. Using cords 9, 10, and 11, tie three square knots. Slide a bead on cords 4 and 8 *(Fig. 3)*.

Fig. 3

7. Repeat Steps 5-6 until the bracelet is the measurement determined in Step 1, ending with square knot groupings.

8. Holding the ends together, tightly wrap a 6" wire length around the cords *(Fig. 4)* close to the knots. Trim the cord ends to $^{1}/_{2}$" long.

Fig. 4

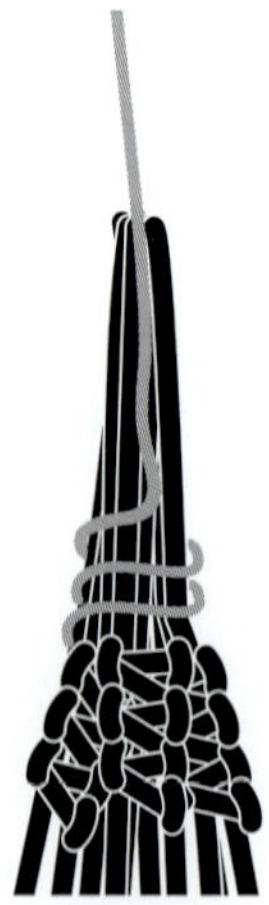

9. Thread the wire end through a cone. Place a generous drop of glue on the cord ends. Pull the wire until the wrapped cord ends are drawn into the cone *(Fig. 5)*. Trim the wire to $^{1}/_{2}$". Make a loop in the wire (page 30).

Fig. 5

10. Untying the overhand knot first, repeat Steps 8-9 for the other end of the bracelet.
11. Use the jump rings (page 30) to attach the toggle clasp to the wire loops.

Jewelry Making Basics

TOOLS

Chain-nose pliers have rounded, tapered jaws and a flat interior surface that will not mar wire. These pliers are used for reaching into tight places, gripping objects, opening and closing jump rings, and bending wire.

Round-nose pliers have round jaws that are useful for making loops and bending wire smoothly.

Wire cutters are used to cut small gauge wire, head pins, and eye pins.

TECHNIQUES

Using a Bead Stop

When threading beads on a thread or cord, you don't want to be concerned that the beads will slide off the other end. A bead stop does just that: it stops the beads from sliding off your beading thread.

You can simply use a larger, different colored bead. Before you start threading on your beads, thread on a bead stop. Run the beading thread or cord around the bead and pass through the bead again, securing it in place *(Fig. 1)*.

Fig. 1

When you are ready to knot the ends, loosen the thread or cord and carefully remove the bead stop. You can now tie a surgeon's knot (page 32).

Chain-Nose Pliers

Round-Nose Pliers

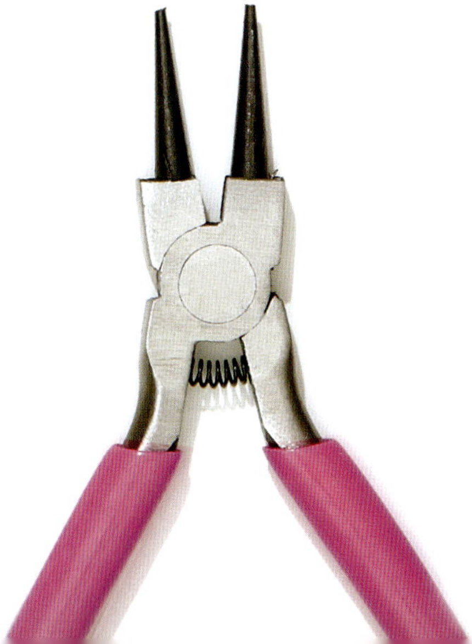

Wire Cutters

Using Jump Rings

Pick up a jump ring with the chain-nose pliers. With a second pair of chain-nose pliers, gently hold the other side of the ring. Open the ring by pulling one pair of pliers toward you while pushing the other away *(Fig. 2)*.

Fig. 2

Close the ring by pushing and pulling the pliers in opposite directions, bringing the ring ends back together.

Making Bead Dangles on Head Pins

Slide your beads on a head pin. Leaving about 1/2", cut off the excess wire. Make a loop on the wire (below).

Making Loops on Wire

Using chain-nose pliers, bend the wire at a 90° angle *(Fig. 3)*. Grasp the very tip of the wire with the round-nose pliers. Turn the pliers and bend the wire into a loop *(Fig. 4)*. Release the pliers. Straighten or twist the loop further if necessary.

Fig. 3

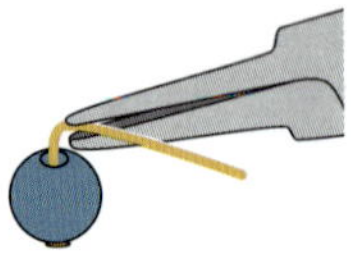

Fig. 4

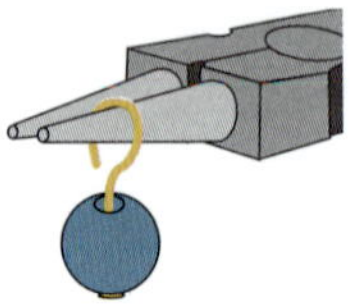

Using Crimp Beads

To finish a wire end, thread a crimp bead and the clasp or jump ring on the wire. Run the wire back through the crimp bead; use a pair of pliers to pull and tighten the wire *(Fig. 5)*. Place the crimp bead on the inner groove of the crimp tool and squeeze *(Fig. 6)*.

Release the tool, turn the crimp bead a quarter turn, and place it in the outer groove *(Fig. 7)*. Squeeze the tool to round out the crimp bead *(Fig. 8)*. Trim the wire end or if the design calls for beads, thread the beads over the wire to cover the end.

Fig. 5

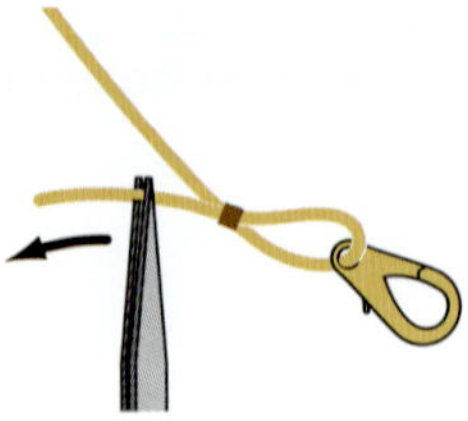

Fig. 6

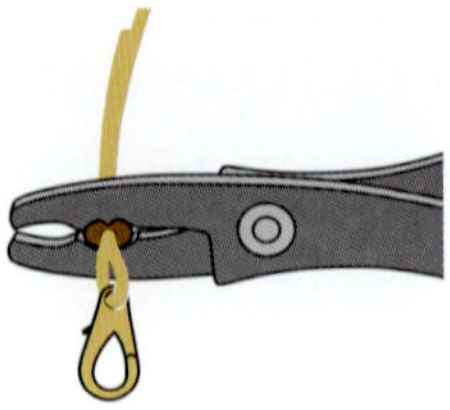

Fig. 7

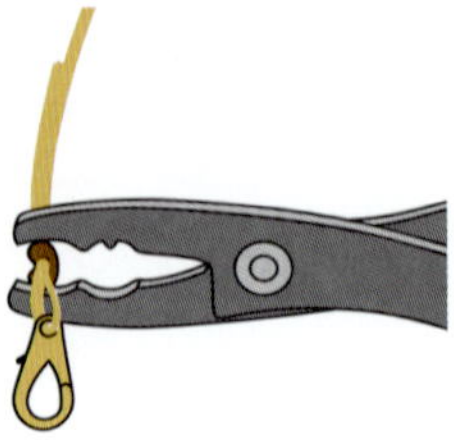

Fig. 8

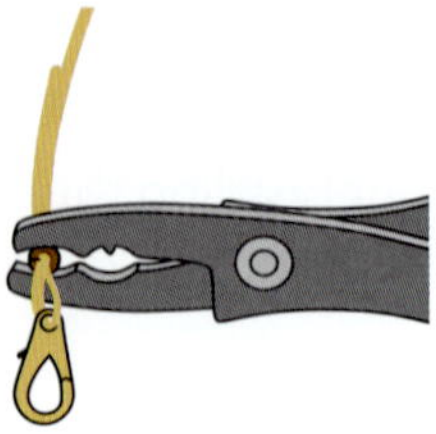

Finishing Cord Ends

Holding the cords together and leaving 1" tails (or tail length given in project instructions), thread the cords through the jump ring or clasp and fold over *(Fig. 9)* or simply fold over to make a loop.

Fig. 9

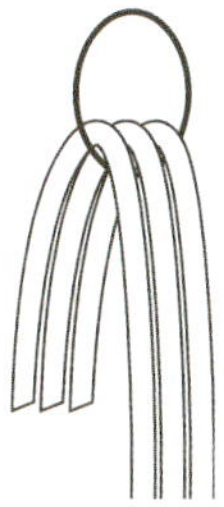

Form a loop with one 12" length of the cord. Wrap the cord around the folded cords 4-5 times. Bring the end through the loop *(Fig. 10)*. Pull firmly on the opposite end of the cord until the loop disappears.

Fig. 10

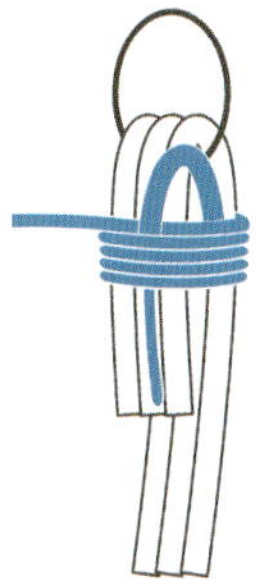

Place a drop of glue on the knot. When the glue is dry, trim the cord ends *(Fig. 11)*.

Fig. 11

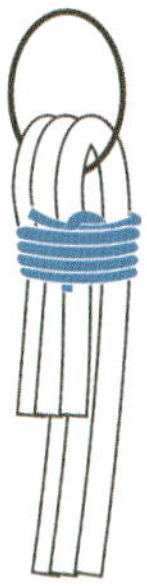

Attaching Foldover Cord Ends

Lay one end of the cord(s) in the foldover cord end. Apply a drop of glue and use the pliers to fold the tabs over the cord(s) *(Fig. 12)*.

Fig. 12

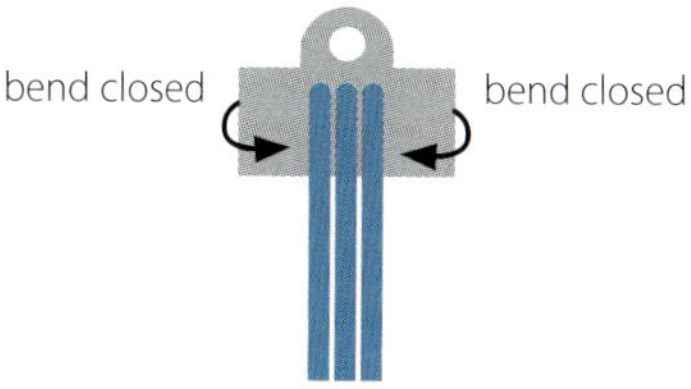

Tying Knots

Lark's Head Knot

Fold the cord in half. Place the loop through the ring, link, or clasp. Bring the cord ends through the loop and pull to tighten *(Fig. 13)*.

Fig. 13

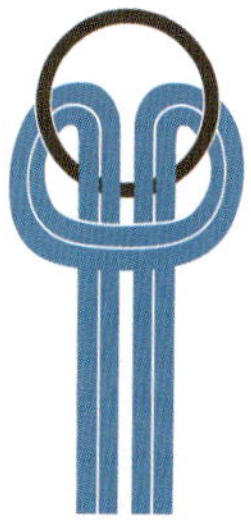

Overhand Knot

For an overhand knot with cut ends, hold the cords together and tie an overhand knot *(Fig. 14)* near one end.

Fig. 14

For an overhand knot with a loop end, fold the cords in half and tie an overhand knot *(Fig. 15)* near the folded end.

Fig. 15

Square Knot

Use the outer cords to tie the first half of a square knot around the center cord(s) *(Fig. 16)*. Tie the second half of the square knot *(Fig. 17)*. When tightening, always pull the cord up or away from you.

Fig. 16

Fig. 17

Surgeon's Knot

Tie a surgeon's knot (Fig. 18) when using stretch cord. Add a drop of jeweler's glue to the knot for extra strength.

Fig. 18

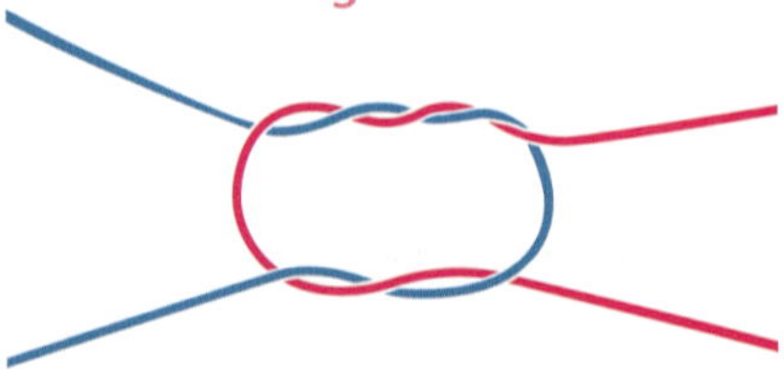

Production Team: Crafts Design Director – Patti Wallenfang; Designer – Kelly Reider; Technical Writer – Lisa Lancaster; Technical Associate – Mary Hutcheson; Editorial Writer – Susan Frantz Wiles; Senior Graphic Artist – Lora Puls; Graphic Artist – Becca Snider Tally; Photostylists – Lori Wenger; Photographers – Jason Masters.